Timeless Learning: Raising Thinkers with Classical Education and AI Innovation

© 2025 by Panthera Uncia Publishing
Edition: 2.7

ISBN: 978-1-0369-1703-6

I0192207

Original Content Copyright

Public Domain Notice for The Lost Tools of Learning

Timeless Learning: Raising Thinkers with Classical Education and AI Innovation

Includes Dorothy L. Sayers': The Lost Tools of Learning

Shoaib Ali Raza & John Branney

Foreword by Irfan H. Latif

PANTHERA UNCIA PUBLISHING

Contents

3: AI as a Thinking Tool, Not a Shortcut

4: Practical Strategies for Parents

5: The Future of Learning is Classical and Technological

Glossary

Acknowledgements

I extend my deepest gratitude to Shaykh Hamza Yusuf, whose insightful lectures first introduced me to Dorothy Sayers' message and the rich traditions of classical education across the world. His work has profoundly shaped my understanding and appreciation of this timeless approach to learning. I am also grateful to Irfan Latif and Simon Mann, whose leadership and thought-provoking discussions have challenged me to explore the intersection of Timeless Learning and emerging technology. Their perspectives have been invaluable in shaping this book. A special thanks to Dr. Fabio Di Salvo and Jozef Bendik for the lively debates in Singapore, which pushed me to examine these ideas. Our conversations have been both inspiring and intellectually stimulating. Thank you to Saba, Mya and Ibby for their continued encouragement. And of course, I'm grateful to my colleague and friend John, who, despite the thousands of miles between us, remains a daily source of knowledge exchange and insight.

Shoaib Ali Raza FRSA

This book is dedicated to all those who believe in the transformative power of teaching. It was my dear friend, Shoaib, who first opened my eyes to the wisdom of Dorothy Sayers and her call to return to the trivium, championing the timeless value of classical learning. I owe a debt of gratitude to Irfan Latif, whose mentorship has been a beacon of inspiration. His wisdom, blending the best of classical and contemporary education, has profoundly influenced my approach to teaching. My heartfelt thanks also go to Anna, Rupert, and Margot, whose unwavering support and encouragement have been a constant source of inspiration, reminding me daily of the importance of building a brighter future. Above all, I am forever grateful to my friend Shoaib, whose relentless pursuit of new ideas and thoughtful challenges has continually pushed me to grow and evolve. Shoaib and I have often discussed how we can shape a system that sparks curiosity, fosters critical thinking, and empowers students to extend their learning beyond the classroom. This book is a testament to the power of collaboration, mentorship, and the shared belief that we can create a better world through education.

John Branney

Foreword

It has been a genuine privilege to know Shoaib and John over many years. As educators, thinkers, and principled innovators, they embody a rare blend of intellectual rigour and deep moral purpose. Their latest work, *Timeless Learning: Raising Thinkers with Classical Education and AI Innovation*, is both a bold provocation and a timely contribution to one of the most urgent conversations in education today.

We find ourselves at a pivotal crossroads. The accelerating impact of artificial intelligence is reshaping how we teach, how we learn, and, perhaps most critically, how we think. Shoaib and John confront this head-on, not with hand-wringing or hype, but with clarity, wisdom, and a deeply rooted educational philosophy. Their central message is simple but profound: while tools may evolve, the timeless purpose of education - cultivating independent thought, intellectual virtue, and moral agency - must remain resolute.

Anchoring their thesis in the enduring insights of Dorothy L. Sayers, they make a compelling case for the return to the classical Trivium -Grammar, Logic, and Rhetoric - as a cognitive framework that can withstand the churn of innovation. Rather than romanticising the past, they ask what we must preserve as we embrace the future. In doing so, they strike a careful balance: they recognise the potential of AI to personalise learning and expand access, while warning of its tendency to encourage what they term "cognitive outsourcing", a subtle erosion of the mental effort, resilience, and reflection that underpin true understanding.

What sets this book apart is not just its diagnosis, but its prescription. Shoaib and John call for a reimagining of the teacher's role, as a designer of learning experiences, as a cultivator of discernment, and as a guide who equips young people to master technology, not be mastered by it. Their insights are as practical as they are principled, offering a roadmap for educators, school leaders, and parents alike.

This is not a book of nostalgia. Nor is it a celebration of uncritical futurism. It is, instead, a courageous invitation to engage with complexity, to hold fast to what matters, and to ensure that education in the age of AI remains deeply and unapologetically human.

Timeless Learning will challenge you, inspire you, and, above all, remind you why education, done well, still has the power to shape not just individuals, but society itself.

Irfan H Latif MA, FRSA, FRSC
Headmaster
The Royal Hospital School, Suffolk, UK

Dorothy Sayers: A Champion of Timeless Learning.

Dorothy L. Sayers (1893-1957) was an extraordinary English writer, scholar, and thinker, best known for her detective fiction, but also celebrated for her profound insights into education and society.

In her influential talk and paper, "The Lost Tools of Learning" (1947), Sayers argued that modern education had lost its way by focusing on delivering content rather than teaching students how to think. She advocated for a return to the classical Trivium: Grammar, Logic (Dialectic), and Rhetoric as a framework for cultivating intellectual virtue and equipping students with the tools of learning.

Sayers was a brilliant and versatile thinker who challenged the educational establishment of her time. Her ideas were radical, advocating for a "progressive retrogression" to the wisdom of the Middle Ages, not to blindly imitate it, but to reclaim its emphasis on the fundamentals of learning. She envisioned an education that cultivates intellectual independence, critical thinking, and the ability to engage with ideas effectively.

Sayers's insights remain profoundly relevant today. Her emphasis on the tools of learning, the cultivation of intellectual virtue, and the importance of active engagement with ideas over passive consumption are crucial in an age of information abundance and technological change. Her work continues to inspire educators and thinkers who seek to cultivate timeless learning in an ever-changing world.

The Lost Tools of Learning

Paper read at a Vacation Course in Education Oxford, 1947 by Dorothy L. Sayers.

The Lost Tools of Learning

That I, whose experience of teaching is extremely limited, and whose life of recent years has been almost wholly out of touch with educational circles, should presume to discuss education is a matter, surely, that calls for no apology. It is a kind of behaviour to which the present climate of opinion is wholly favourable. Bishops air their opinions about economics; biologists, about metaphysics; celibates, about matrimony; inorganic chemists, about theology; the most irrelevant people are appointed to highly technical ministries; and plain, blunt men write to the papers to say that Epstein and Picasso do not know how to draw. Up to a certain point, and provided that the criticisms are made with a reasonable modesty, these activities are commendable. Too much specialisation is not a good thing. There is also one excellent reason why the veriest amateur may feel entitled to have an opinion about education. For if we are not all professional teachers, we have all, at some time or other, been taught. Even if we learnt nothing (perhaps in particular if we learnt nothing), our contribution to the discussion may have a potential value.

Without apology, then, I will begin. But since much that I have to say is highly controversial, it will be pleasant to start with a proposition with which, I feel confident, all teachers will cordially agree; and that is, that they all work much too hard and have far too many things to do. One has only to look at any school or examination syllabus to see that it is cluttered up with a great variety of exhausting subjects which they are called upon to teach, and the teaching of which sadly interferes with what every thoughtful mind will allow to be their proper duties, such as distributing milk, supervising meals, taking cloakroom duty, weighing and measuring pupils, keeping their eyes open for incipient mumps, measles and chickenpox, making out lists, escorting parties round the Victoria and Albert Museum, filling up forms, interviewing parents, and devising end-of-term reports which shall combine a deep veneration for truth with a tender respect for the feelings of all concerned.

Upon these really important duties I will not enlarge. I propose only to deal with the subject of teaching, properly so-called. I want to inquire whether, amid all the multitudinous subjects which figure in the syllabuses, we are really teaching the right things in the right way; and whether, by teaching fewer things, differently, we might not succeed in "shedding the load" (as the fashionable phrase goes) and, at the same time, producing a better result.

This prospect need arouse neither hope nor alarm. It is in the highest degree improbable that the reforms I propose will ever be carried into effect. Neither the parents, nor the training colleges, nor the examination boards, nor the boards of governors, nor the Ministry of Education would countenance them for a moment. For they amount to this: that if we are to produce a society of educated people, fitted to preserve their intellectual freedom amid the complex pressures of our modern society, we must turn back the wheel of progress some four or five hundred years, to the point at which education began to lose sight of its true object, towards the end of the Middle Ages.

Before you dismiss me with the appropriate phrase (reactionary, romantic, mediaevalist, laudator temporis acti, or whatever tag comes first to hand), I will ask you to consider one or two miscellaneous questions that hang about at the back, perhaps, of all our minds, and occasionally pop out to worry us.

When we think about the remarkably early age at which the young men went up to the University in, let us say, Tudor times, and thereafter were held fit to assume responsibility for the conduct of their own affairs, are we altogether comfortable about that artificial prolongation of intellectual childhood and adolescence into the years of physical maturity which is so marked in our own day? To postpone the acceptance of responsibility to a late date brings with it a number of psychological complications which, while they may interest the psychiatrist, are scarcely beneficial either to the individual or to society. The stock argument in favour of postponing the school leaving- age and prolonging the period of education generally is that there is now so much more to learn than there was in the Middle Ages. This is partly true, but not wholly.

The modern boy and girl are certainly taught more subjects, but does that always mean that they are actually more learned and know more? That is the very point which we are going to consider.

Has it ever struck you as odd, or unfortunate, that to-day, when the proportion of literacy throughout Western Europe is higher than it has ever been, people should have become susceptible to the influence of advertisement and mass-propaganda to an extent hitherto unheard-of and unimagined? Do you put this down to the mere mechanical fact that the press and the radio and so on have made propaganda much easier to distribute over a wide area? Or do you sometimes have an uneasy suspicion that the product of modern educational methods is less good than he or she might be at disentangling fact from opinion and the proven from the plausible?

Have you ever, in listening to a debate among adult and presumably responsible people, been fretted by the extraordinary inability of the average debater to speak to the question, or to meet and refute the arguments of speakers on the other side? Or have you ever pondered upon the extremely high incidence of irrelevant matter which crops up at committee-meetings, and upon the very great rarity of persons capable of acting as chairmen of committees? And when you think of this, and think that most of our public affairs are settled by debates and committees, have you ever felt a certain sinking of the heart? Have you ever followed a discussion in the newspapers or elsewhere and noticed how frequently writers fail to define the terms they use? Or how often, if one man does define his terms, another will assume in his reply that he was using the terms in precisely the opposite sense to that in which he has already defined them?

Have you ever been faintly troubled by the amount of slipshod syntax going about? And if so, are you troubled because it is inelegant or because it may lead to dangerous misunderstanding?

Do you ever find that young people, when they have left school, not only forget most of what they have learnt (that is only to be expected) but forget also, or betray that they have never really known, how to tackle a new subject for themselves? Are you often bothered by coming across grown-up men and women who seem unable to distinguish between a book that is sound, scholarly and properly documented, and one that is to any trained eye, very conspicuously none of these things? Or who cannot handle a library catalogue? Or who, when faced with a book of reference, betray a curious inability to extract from it the passages relevant to the particular question which interests them?

Do you often come across people for whom, all their lives, a "subject" remains a "subject," divided by watertight bulkheads from all other "subjects," so that they experience very great difficulty in making an immediate mental connection between, let us say, algebra and detective fiction, sewage disposal and the price of salmon, cellulose and the distribution of rainfall, or, more generally, between such spheres of knowledge as philosophy and economics, or chemistry and art?

Are you occasionally perturbed by the things written by adult men and women for adult men and women to read? Here, for instance, is a quotation from an evening paper. It refers to the visit of an Indian girl to this country:

Miss Bhosle has a perfect command of English ("Oh, gosh," she said once), and a marked enthusiasm for London.

Well, we may all talk nonsense in a moment of inattention. It is more alarming when we find a well-known biologist writing in a weekly paper to the effect that: "It is an argument against the existence of a Creator" (I think he put it more strongly; but since I have, most unfortunately, mislaid the reference, I will put his claim at its lowest). He stated that it is an argument against the existence of a Creator that the same kind of variations which are produced by natural selection can be produced at will by stock-breeders. One might feel tempted to say that it is rather an argument for the existence of a Creator. Actually, of course, it is neither. All it proves is that the same material causes (recombination of the chromosomes by cross-breeding and so forth) are sufficient to account for all observed variations, just as the various combinations of the same 13 semitones are materially sufficient to account for Beethoven's Moonlight Sonata and the noise the cat makes by walking on the keys. But the cat's

13

performance neither proves nor disproves the existence of Beethoven; and all that is proved by the biologist's argument is that he was unable to distinguish between a material and a final cause.

Here is a sentence from no less academic a source than a front-page article in the Times Literary Supplement:

> The Frenchman, Alfred Epinas, pointed out that certain species (e.g., ants and wasps) can only face the horrors of life and death in association.

I do not know what the Frenchman actually did say; what the Englishman says he said is patently meaningless. We cannot know whether life holds any horror for the ant, nor in what sense the isolated wasp which you kill upon the windowpane can be said to "face" or not to "face" the horrors of death. The subject of the article is mass behaviour in man, and the human motives have been unobtrusively transferred from the main proposition to the supporting instance. Thus, the argument, in effect, assumes what it sets out to prove. This would become immediately apparent if it were presented in a formal syllogism. This is only a small and haphazard example of a vice that pervades whole books, particularly books written by men of science on metaphysical subjects.

Another quotation from the same issue of the T.L.S. comes in fittingly here to wind up this random collection of disquieting thoughts this time from a review of Sir Richard Livingstone's Some Tasks for Education:

> More than once the reader is reminded of the value of an intensive study of at least one subject, so as to learn "the meaning of knowledge" and what precision and persistence is needed to attain it. Yet

there is else where full recognition of the distressing fact that a man may be master in one field and show no better judgment than his neighbour anywhe else; he remembers what he has learnt, but forgets altogether how he learned it.

I would draw your attention particularly to that last sentence, which offers an explanation of what the writer rightly calls the "distressing fact" that the intellectual skills bestowed upon us by our education are not readily transferable to subjects other than those in which we acquired them: "he remembers what he has learnt, but forgets altogether how he learned it."

Is it not the great defect of our education today (a defect traceable through all the disquieting symptoms of trouble that I have mentioned), that although we often succeed in teaching our pupils "subjects," we fail lamentably on the whole in teaching them how to think? They learn everything except the art of learning. It is as though we had taught a child, mechanically and by rule of thumb, to play The Harmonious Blacksmith upon the piano, but had never taught him the scale or how to read music; so that, having memorised The Harmonious Blacksmith, he still had not the faintest notion how to proceed from that to tackle The Last Rose of Summer. Why do I say "as though"? In certain of the arts and crafts, we sometimes do precisely this: requiring a child to "express himself" in paint before we teach him how to handle the colours and the brush. There is a school of thought which believes this to be the right way to set about the job. But observe, it is not the way in which a trained craftsman will go about to teach himself a new medium. He, having learned by experience the best way to economise labour and take the thing by the right end, will start off by doodling about on an odd piece of material in order to "give himself the feel of the tool."

Let us now look at the mediæval scheme of education, the syllabus of the schools. It does not matter, for the moment, whether it was devised for small children or for older students, or how long people were supposed to take over it. What matters is the light it throws upon what the men of the Middle Ages supposed to be the object and the right order of the educative process. The syllabus was divided into two parts: the Trivium and the Quadrivium. The second part, the Quadrivium, consisted of "subjects," and need not concern us for the moment. The interesting thing for us is the composition of the Trivium, which preceded the Quadrivium and was the preliminary discipline for it. It consisted of three parts: Grammar, Dialectic, and Rhetoric, in that order.

Now the first thing we notice is that two, at any rate, of these "subjects" are not what we should call "subjects" at all; they are only methods of dealing with subjects. Grammar, indeed, is a "subject" in the sense that it does mean definitely learning a language. At that period, it meant learning Latin. But language itself is simply the medium in which thought is expressed. The whole of the Trivium was, in fact, intended to teach the pupil the proper use of the tools of learning before he began to apply them to "subjects" at all.

First, he learned a language. Not just how to order a meal in a foreign language, but the structure of language, the nature of a language, and hence of language itself: what it was, how it was put together, and how it worked. Secondly, he learned how to use language: how to define his terms and make accurate statements, how to construct an argument, and how to detect fallacies in argument, his own and other people's. Dialectic, that is to say, embraced Logic and Disputation. Thirdly, he learned to express himself in language: how to say what he had to say elegantly and persuasively. At this point, any tendency to express himself windily or to use his eloquence to make the worse appear the better reason would, no doubt, be restrained by his previous teaching in Dialectic.

16

If not, his teacher and his fellow-pupils, trained along the same lines, would be quick to point out where he was wrong, for it was they whom he had to seek to persuade. At the end of his course, he was required to compose a thesis upon some theme set by his masters or chosen by himself, and afterwards to defend his thesis against the criticism of the faculty. By this time he would have learned, or woe betide him, not merely to write an essay on paper but to speak audibly and intelligibly from a platform and to use his wits quickly when heckled. The heckling, moreover, would not consist solely of offensive personalities or of irrelevant queries about what Julius Cæsar said in 55 B.C., though no doubt mediæval dialectic was enlivened in practice by plenty of such primitive repartee. But there would also be questions, cogent and shrewd, from those who had already run the gauntlet of debate or were making ready to run it.

It is, of course, quite true that bits and pieces of the mediæval tradition still linger, or have been revived, in the ordinary school syllabus of today. Some knowledge of grammar is still required when learning a foreign language, perhaps I should say "is again required," for during my own lifetime we passed through a phase when the teaching of declensions and conjugations was considered rather reprehensible, and it was considered better to pick these things up as we went along. School debating societies flourish; essays are written; the necessity for "self-expression" is stressed, and perhaps even over-stressed. But these activities are cultivated more or less in detachment, as belonging to the special subjects in which they are pigeon-holed rather than as forming one coherent scheme of mental training to which all "subjects" stand in a subordinate relation. "Grammar" belongs especially to the "subject" of foreign languages, and essay-writing to the "subject" called "English," while Dialectic has become almost entirely divorced from the rest of the curriculum and is frequently practiced unsystematically and out of school-hours as a separate exercise, only very loosely related to the main business of learning. Taken by and large, the great difference of emphasis between the two conceptions holds good: modern education concentrates on teaching subjects, leaving the method of thinking, arguing, and expressing one's conclusions to be picked up by the scholar as he goes along; mediæval education concentrated on first *forging and learning* to handle the tools of learning, using whatever subject came handy as a piece of material on which to doodle until the use of the tool became second nature.

"Subjects" of some kind there must be, of course. One cannot learn the use of a tool by merely waving it in the air; neither can one learn the theory of grammar without learning an actual language, or learn to argue and orate without speaking about something in particular. The debating subjects of the Middle Ages were drawn largely from Theology, or from the Ethics and History of Antiquity. Often, indeed, they became stereotyped, especially towards the end of the period; and the far-fetched and wire-drawn absurdities of scholastic argument fretted Milton and provide food for merriment even to this day. Whether they were in themselves any more hackneyed and trivial than the usual subjects set nowadays for "essay-writing" I should not like to say: we may ourselves grow a little weary of "A Day in My Holidays," "What I should Like to Do when I Leave School," and all the rest of it. But most of the merriment is misplaced, because the aim and object of the debating thesis has by now been lost sight of. A glib speaker in the Brains Trust once entertained his audience (and reduced the late Charles Williams to helpless rage) by asserting that in the Middle Ages it was a matter of faith to know how many archangels could dance on the point of a needle. I need not say, I hope, that it never was a "matter of faith"; it was simply a debating exercise, whose set subject was the nature of angelic substance: were angels material, and if so, did they occupy space? The answer usually adjudged correct is, I believe, that angels are pure intelligences; not material, but limited, so that they may have location in space but not extension.

An analogy might be drawn from human thought, which is similarly non-material and similarly limited. Thus, if your thought is concentrated upon one thing, say the point of a needle, it is located there in the sense that it is not elsewhere. But although it is "there," it occupies no space there, and there is nothing to prevent an infinite number of different people's thoughts being concentrated upon the same needle point at the same time. The proper subject of the argument is thus seen to be the distinction between location and extension in space; the matter on which the argument is exercised happens to be the nature of angels (although, as we have seen, it might equally well have been something else). The practical lesson to be drawn from the argument is not to use words like "there" in a loose and unscientific way, without specifying whether you mean "located there" or "occupying space there." Scorn in plenty has been poured out upon the mediæval passion for hair-splitting, but when we look at the shameless abuse made, in print and on the platform, of controversial expressions with shifting and ambiguous connotations, we may feel it in our hearts to wish that every reader and hearer had been so defensively armored by his education as to be able to cry: Distinguo.

For we let our young men and women go out unarmed, in a day when armour was never so necessary. By teaching them all to read, we have left them at the mercy of the printed word. By the invention of the film and the radio, we have made certain that no aversion to reading shall secure them from the incessant battery of words, words, words. They do not know what the words mean; they do not know how to ward them off or blunt their edge or fling them back; they are a prey to words in their emotions instead of being the masters of them in their intellects. We who were scandalised in 1940 when men were sent to fight armoured tanks with rifles are not scandalised when young men and women are sent into the world to fight massed propaganda with a smattering of "subjects." And when whole classes and whole nations become hypnotised by the arts of the spellbinder, we have the impudence to be astonished. We give only lip service to the importance of education, lip service and, just occasionally, a little grant of money. We postpone the school leaving age and plan to build bigger and better schools. The teachers slave conscientiously in and out of school hours until responsibility becomes a burden and a nightmare; and yet, as I believe, all this devoted effort is largely frustrated because we have lost the tools of learning and in their absence can only make a botched and piecemeal job of it.

What, then, are we to do? We cannot go back to the Middle Ages. That is a cry to which we have become accustomed. We cannot go back or can we? Distinguo. I should like every term in that proposition defined. Does "Go back" mean a retrogression in time or the revision of an error? The first is clearly impossible per se; the second is a thing which wise men do every day. Does "Cannot" mean that our behaviour is determined by some irreversible cosmic mechanism or merely that such an action would be very difficult in view of the opposition it would provoke? "The Middle Ages" obviously is not and cannot be the fourteenth century; but if "the Middle Ages" is, in this context, simply a picturesque phrase denoting a particular educational theory, there seems to be no a priori reason why we should not "go back" to it with modifications as we have already "gone back" to it, with modifications, to, let us say, the idea of playing Shakespeare's plays as he wrote them, and not in the "modernised" versions of Cibber and Garrick, which once seemed to be the latest thing in theatrical progress.

Let us amuse ourselves by imagining that such progressive retrogression is possible. Let us make a clean sweep of all educational authorities and furnish ourselves with a nice little school of boys and girls whom we may experimentally equip for the intellectual conflict along lines chosen by ourselves. We will endow them with exceptionally docile parents. We will staff our school with teachers who are themselves perfectly familiar with the aims and methods of the Trivium. We will have our buildings and staff large enough to allow our classes to be small enough for adequate handling, and we will postulate a Board of Examiners willing and qualified to test the products we turn out. Thus prepared, we will attempt to sketch out a syllabus, a modern Trivium "with modifications," and we will see where we get to.

But first: what age shall the children be? Well, if one is to educate them on novel lines, it will be better that they should have nothing to unlearn; besides, one cannot begin a good thing too early, and the Trivium is by its nature not learning, but a preparation for learning. We will therefore "catch 'em young," requiring only of our pupils that they shall be able to read, write and cipher.

My views about child psychology are, I admit, neither orthodox nor enlightened. Looking back upon myself (since I am the child I know best and the only child I can pretend to know from inside) I recognise in myself three states of development. These, in a rough-and-ready fashion, I will call the Poll-parrot, the Pert, and the Poetic, the latter coinciding, approximately, with the onset of puberty. The Poll-parrot stage is the one in which learning by heart is easy and, on the whole, pleasurable, whereas reasoning is difficult and, on the whole, little relished. At this age one readily memorises the shapes and appearances of things; one likes to recite the number-plates of cars; one rejoices in the chanting of rhymes and the rumble and thunder of unintelligible polysyllables; one enjoys the mere accumulation of things. The Pert Age, which follows upon this (and, naturally, overlaps it to some extent) is only too familiar to all who have to do with children: it is characterised by contradicting, answering-back, liking to "catch people out" (especially one's elders), and the propounding of conundrums (especially the kind with a nasty verbal catch in them). Its nuisance-value is extremely high. It usually sets in about the Lower Fourth. The Poetic Age is popularly known as the "difficult" age. It is self-centered; it yearns to express itself; it rather specialises in being misunderstood; it is restless and tries to achieve independence; and, with good luck and good guidance, it should show the beginnings of creativeness, a reaching-out towards a synthesis of what it already knows, and a deliberate eagerness to know and do some one thing in preference to all others. Now it seems to me that the lay-out of the Trivium adapts itself with a singular appropriateness to these three ages: Grammar to the Poll-parrot, Dialectic to the Pert, and Rhetoric to the Poetic Age.

Let us begin, then, with Grammar. This, in practice, means the grammar of some language in particular; and it must be an inflected language. The grammatical structure of an uninflected language is far too analytical to be tackled by any one without previous practice in Dialectic. Moreover, the inflected languages interpret the uninflected, whereas the uninflected are of little use in interpreting the inflected. I will say at once, quite firmly, that the best grounding for education is the Latin grammar. I say this, not because Latin is traditional and mediæval, but simply because even a rudimentary knowledge of Latin cuts down the labor and pains of learning almost any other subject by at least 50 percent. It is the key to the vocabulary and structure of all the Romance languages and to the structure of all the Teutonic languages, as well as to the technical vocabulary of all the sciences and to the literature of the entire Mediterranean civilisation, together with all its historical documents. Those whose pedantic preference for a living language persuades them to deprive their pupils of all these advantages might substitute Russian, whose grammar is still more primitive. (The verb is complicated by a number of "aspects," and I rather fancy that it enjoys three complete voices and a couple of extra aorists, but I may be thinking of Basque or Sanskrit.) Russian is, of course, helpful with the other Slav dialects. There is something also to be said for classical Greek. But my own choice is Latin. Having thus pleased the Classicists, I will proceed to horrify them by adding that I do not think it either wise or necessary to cramp the ordinary pupil upon the Procrustean bed of the Augustan Age with its highly elaborate and artificial verse forms and oratory. The post-classical and mediæval Latin, which was a living language down to the end of the Renaissance, is easier and in some ways livelier, both in syntax and rhythm; and a study of it helps to dispel the widespread notion that learning and literature came to a full stop when Christ was born and only woke up again at the Dissolution of the Monasteries.

However, I am running ahead too fast. We are still in the grammatical stage. Latin should be begun as early as possible at a time when inflected speech seems no more astonishing than any other phenomenon in an astonishing world, and when the chanting of "amo, amas, amat" is as ritually agreeable to the feelings as the chanting of "eeny, meeny, miney, mo."

During this age we must, of course, exercise the mind on other things besides Latin grammar. Observation and memory are the faculties most lively at this period; and if we are to learn a contemporary foreign language we should begin now, before the facial and mental muscles become rebellious to strange intonations. Spoken French or German can be practised alongside the grammatical discipline of the Latin.

In English, verse and prose can be learned by heart, and the pupil's memory should be stored with stories of every kind, classical myth, European legend, and so forth. I do not think that the Classical stories and masterpieces of ancient literature should be made the vile bodies on which to practise the technics of Grammar; that was a fault of mediæval education which we need not perpetuate. The stories can be enjoyed and remembered in English, and related to their origin at a subsequent stage. Recitation aloud should be practiced, individually or in chorus, for we must not forget that we are laying the groundwork for Disputation and Rhetoric.

The grammar of History should consist, I think, of dates, events, anecdotes, and personalities. A set of dates to which one can peg all later historical knowledge is of enormous help later on in establishing the perspective of history. It does not greatly matter which dates: those of the Kings of England will do very nicely, provided they are accompanied by pictures of costume, architecture, and all "every-day things," so that the mere mention of a date calls up a strong visual presentment of the whole period.

Geography will similarly be presented in its factual aspect, with maps, natural features and visual presentment of customs, costumes, flora, fauna, and so on; and I believe myself that the discredited and old-fashioned memorising of a few capital cities, rivers, mountain ranges, etc., does no harm. Stamp-collecting may be encouraged.

Science, in the Poll-parrot period, arranges itself naturally and easily round collections, the identifying and naming of specimens and, in general, the kind of thing that used to be called "natural history," or, still more charmingly, "natural philosophy." To know the names and properties of things is, at this age, a satisfaction in itself: to recognise a devil's coach-horse at sight, and assure one's foolish elders that, in spite of its appearance, it does not sting; to be able to pick out Cassiopeia and the Pleiades, and possibly even to know who Cassiopeia and the Pleiades were; to be aware that a whale is not a fish, and a bat not a bird. All these things give a pleasant sensation of superiority, while to know a ring-snake from an adder or a poisonous from an edible toadstool is a kind of knowledge that has also a practical value.

The grammar of *Mathematics* begins, of course, with the multiplication table, which, if not learnt now, will never be learnt with pleasure; and with the recognition of geometrical shapes and the grouping of numbers. These exercises lead naturally to the doing of simple sums in arithmetic; and if the pupil shows a bent that way, a facility acquired at this stage is all to the good. More complicated mathematical processes may, and perhaps should, be postponed, for reasons which will presently appear.

So far (except, of course, for the Latin), our curriculum contains nothing that departs very far from common practice. The difference will be felt rather in the attitude of the teachers, who must look upon all these activities less as "subjects" in themselves than as a gathering together of material for use in the next part of the Trivium. What that material actually is is only of secondary importance, but it is as well that anything and everything which can usefully be committed to memory should be memorised at this period, whether it is immediately intelligible or not. The modern tendency is to try and force rational explanations on a child's mind at too early an age. Intelligent questions, spontaneously asked, should, of course, receive an immediate and rational answer, but it is a great mistake to suppose that a child cannot readily enjoy and remember things that are beyond its power to analyse, particularly if those things have a strong imaginative appeal (as, for example, Kubla Khan), an attractive jingle (like some of the memory rhymes for Latin genders), or an abundance of rich, resounding polysyllables (like the Quicunque Vult).

This reminds me of the Grammar of Theology. I shall add it to the curriculum, because Theology is the Mistress-science, without which the whole educational structure will necessarily lack its final synthesis. Those who disagree about this will remain content to leave their pupils' education still full of loose ends. This will matter rather less than it might, since by the time that the tools of learning have been forged the student will be able to tackle Theology for himself, and will probably insist upon doing so and making sense of it. Still, it is as well to have this matter also handy and ready for the reason to work upon. At the grammatical age, therefore, we should become acquainted with the story of God and Man in outline, i.e., the Old and New Testament presented as parts of a single narrative of Creation, Rebellion, and

and Redemption, and also with "the Creed, the Lord's Prayer, and the Ten Commandments." At this stage, it does not matter nearly so much that these things should be fully understood as that they should be known and remembered. Remember, it is material that we are collecting.

It is difficult to say at what age, precisely, we should pass from the first to the second part of the Trivium. Generally speaking, the answer is: so soon as the pupil shows himself disposed to Pertness and interminable argument (or, as a school-master correspondent of mine more elegantly puts it: "When the capacity for abstract thought begins to manifest itself"). For as, in the first part, the master-faculties are Observation and Memory, so in the second, the master-faculty is the Discursive Reason. In the first, the exercise to which the rest of the material was, as it were, keyed, was the Latin Grammar; in the second the key-exercise will be Formal Logic. It is here that our curriculum shows its first sharp divergence from modern standards. The disrepute into which Formal Logic has fallen is entirely unjustified; and its neglect is the root cause of nearly all those disquieting symptoms which we may note in the modern intellectual constitution. Logic has been discredited, partly because we have fallen into a habit of supposing that we are conditioned almost entirely by the intuitive and the unconscious. There is no time now to argue whether this is true; I will content myself with observing that to neglect the proper training of the reason is the best possible way to make it true, and to ensure the supremacy of the intuitive, irrational and unconscious elements in our make-up. A secondary cause for the disfavour into which Formal Logic has fallen is the belief that it is entirely based upon universal assumptions that are either unprovable or tautological. This is not true. Not all universal propositions are of this kind. But even if they were, it would make no difference, since every syllogism whose major premise is in the form "All A is B" can be recast in can be recast in hypothetical form. Logic is the art of arguing correctly: "If A, then B"; the method is not invalidated by the hypothetical character of A. Indeed, the practical utility of Formal Logic to-day lies not so much in the establishment of positive conclusions as in the prompt detection and exposure of invalid inference.

Let us now quickly review our material and see how it is to be related to Dialectic. On the *Language* side, we shall now have our Vocabulary and Morphology at our finger-tips; henceforward we can concentrate more particularly on Syntax and Analysis (*i.e.*, the logical construction of speech) and the history of Language (*i.e.*, how we come to arrange our speech as we do in order to convey our thoughts).

Our Reading will proceed from narrative and lyric to essays, argument and criticism, and the pupil will learn to try his own hand at writing this kind of thing. Many lessons on whatever subject will take the form of debates; and the place of individual or choral recitation will be taken by dramatic performances, with special attention to plays in which an argument is stated in dramatic form.

Mathematics, Algebra, Geometry, and the more advanced kind of Arithmetic will now enter into the syllabus and take its place as what it really is: not a separate "subject" but a sub-department of Logic. It is neither more nor less than the rule of the syllogism in its particular application to number and measurement, and should be taught as such, instead of being, for some, a dark mystery, and for others, a special revelation, neither illuminating nor illuminated by any other part of knowledge.

History, aided by a simple system of ethics derived from the Grammar of Theology, will provide much suitable material for discussion. Was the behaviour of this statesman justified? What was the effect of such an enactment? What are the arguments for and against this or that form of government? We shall thus get an introduction to constitutional History, a subject meaningless to the young child but of absorbing interest to those who are prepared to argue and debate. Theology itself will furnish material for argument about conduct and morals, and should have its scope extended by a simplified course of dogmatic theology (i.e., the rational structure of Christian thought), clarifying the relations between the dogma and the ethics, and lending itself to that application of ethical principles in particular instances which is properly called casuistry. Geography and the Sciences will all likewise provide material for Dialectic.

Theology itself will furnish material for argument about conduct and morals; and should have its scope extended by a simplified course of dogmatic theology (i.e., the rational structure of Christian thought), clarifying the relations between the dogma and the ethics, and lending itself to that application of ethical principles in particular instances which is properly called casuistry. Geography and the Sciences will all likewise provide material for Dialectic.

But above all, we must not neglect the material which is so abundant in the pupils' own daily life. There is a delightful passage in Leslie Paul's The Living Hedge which tells how a number of small boys enjoyed themselves for days arguing about an extraordinary shower of rain which had fallen in their town, a shower so localised that it left one half of the main street wet and the other dry. Could one, they argued, properly say that it had rained that day on or over the town, or only in the town? How many drops of water were required to constitute rain? And so on. Argument about this led on to a host of similar problems about rest and motion, sleep and waking, est and non est, and the infinitesimal division of time. The whole passage is an admirable example of the spontaneous development of the ratiocinative faculty and the natural and proper thirst of the awakening reason for definition of terms and exactness of statement. All events are food for such an appetite. An umpire's decision, the degree to which one may transgress the spirit of a regulation without being trapped by the letter, on such questions as these, children are born casuists, and their natural propensity only needs to be developed and trained, especially brought into an intelligible relationship with events in the grown-up world. The newspapers are full of good material for such exercises: legal decisions, on the one hand, in cases where the cause at issue is not too abstruse; on the other, fallacious reasoning and muddle-headed argument, with which the correspondence columns of certain papers one could name are abundantly stocked.

Wherever the matter for Dialectic is found, it is, of course, highly important that attention should be focused upon the beauty and economy of a fine demonstration or a well-turned argument, lest veneration should wholly die. Criticism must not be merely destructive; though at the same time both teacher and pupils must be ready to detect fallacy, slipshod reasoning, ambiguity, irrelevance, and redundancy, and to pounce upon them like rats.

This is the moment when précis-writing may be usefully undertaken; together with such exercises as the writing of an essay, and the reduction of it, when written, by 25 or 50 percent.

It will doubtless be objected that to encourage young persons at the Pert Age to browbeat, correct, and argue with their elders will render them perfectly intolerable. My answer is that children of that age are intolerable anyhow; and that their natural argumentativeness may just as well be canalised to good purpose as allowed to run away into the sands. It may, indeed, be rather less obtrusive at home if it is disciplined in school; and, anyhow, elders who have abandoned the wholesome principle that children should be seen and not heard have no one to blame but themselves. The teachers, to be sure, will have to mind their step, or they may get more than they bargained for. All children sit in judgment on their masters; and if the Chaplain's sermon or the Headmistress's annual Speech-day address should by any chance afford an opening for the point of the critical wedge, that wedge will go home the more forcibly under the weight of the Dialectical hammer, wielded by a practised hand. That is why I said that the teachers themselves would have to have undergone the discipline of the Trivium before they set out to impose it on their charges.

Once again: the contents of the syllabus at this stage may be anything you like. The "subjects" supply material; but they are all to be regarded as mere grist for the mental mill to work upon. The pupils should be encouraged to go and forage for their own information, and so guided towards the proper use of libraries and books of reference, and shown how to tell which sources are authoritative and which are not.

Towards the close of this stage, the pupils will probably be beginning to discover for themselves that their knowledge and experience are insufficient, and that their trained intelligences need a great deal more material to chew upon. The imagination, usually dormant during the Pert Age, will reawaken and prompt them to suspect the limitations of logic and reason. This means that they are passing into the

Poetic Age and are ready to embark on the study of Rhetoric. The doors of the storehouse of knowledge should now be thrown open for them to browse about as they will. The things once learned by rote will now be seen in new contexts; the things once coldly analyzed can now be brought together to form a new synthesis; here and there a sudden insight will bring about that most exciting of all discoveries: the realisation that a truism is true.

It is difficult to map out any general syllabus for the study of Rhetoric: a certain freedom is demanded. In literature, appreciation should be again allowed to take the lead over destructive criticism; and self-expression in writing can go forward, with its tools now sharpened to cut clean and observe proportion. Any child that already shows a disposition to specialise should be given his head: for, when the use of the tools has been well and truly learned it is available for any study whatever. It would be well, I think, that each pupil should learn to do one, or two, subjects really well, while taking a few classes in subsidiary subjects so as to keep his mind open to the inter-relations of all knowledge. Indeed, at this stage, our difficulty will be to keep "subjects" apart; for as Dialectic will have shown all branches of learning to be inter-related, so Rhetoric will tend to show that all knowledge is one. To show this, and show why it is so, is pre-eminently the task of the Mistress-science. But whether Theology is studied or not, we should at least insist that children who seem inclined to specialise on the mathematical and scientific side should be obliged to attend some lessons in the Humanities and vice versâ. At this stage also, the Latin Grammar, having done its work, may be dropped for those who prefer to carry on their language studies on the modern side; while those who are likely never to have any great use or aptitude for mathematics might also be allowed to rest, more or less, upon their oars. Generally speaking: whatsoever is mere apparatus may now be allowed to fall into the background, while the trained mind is gradually prepared for specialisation in the "subjects" which, when the Trivium is completed, it should be perfectly well equipped to tackle on its own. The final synthesis of the Trivium, the presentation and public defence of the thesis, should be restored in some form; perhaps as a kind of "leaving examination" during the last term at school.

The scope of Rhetoric depends also on whether the pupil is to be turned out into the world at the age of sixteen or whether he is to proceed to public school and/or university. Since, really, Rhetoric should be taken at about fourteen, the first category of pupil should study Grammar from about nine to eleven, and Dialectic from twelve to fourteen; his last two school years would then be devoted to Rhetoric, which, in his case, would be of a fairly specialized and vocational kind, suiting him to enter immediately upon some practical career. A pupil of the second category would finish his Dialectical course in his Preparatory School, and take Rhetoric during his first two years at his Public School. At sixteen, he would be ready to start upon those "subjects" which are proposed for his later study at the university; and this part of his education will correspond to the mediæval Quadrivium. What this amounts to is that the ordinary pupil, whose formal education ends at sixteen, will take the Trivium only; whereas scholars will take both Trivium and Quadrivium.

Is the Trivium, then, a sufficient education for life? Properly taught, I believe that it should be. At the end of the Dialectic, the children will probably seem to be far behind their coevals brought up on old-fashioned "modern" methods, so far as detailed knowledge of specific subjects is concerned. But after the age of fourteen they should be able to overhaul the others hand over fist. Indeed, I am not at all sure that a pupil thoroughly proficient in the Trivium would not be fit to proceed immediately to the university at the age of sixteen, thus proving himself the equal of his mediæval counterpart, whose precocity often appears to us so astonishing and unaccountable. This, to be sure, would make hay of the public-school system, and disconcert the universities very much. It would, for example, make quite a different thing of the Oxford and Cambridge Boat-race. But I am not now considering the feelings of academic bodies: I am concerned only with the proper training of the mind to encounter and deal with the formidable mass of undigested problems presented to it by the modern world. For the tools of learning are the same, in any and every subject; and the person who knows how to use them will, at any age, get the mastery of a new subject in half the time and with a quarter of the effort expended by the person who has not the tools at his command. To learn six subjects without remembering how they were learnt does nothing to ease the approach to a seventh; to have learnt and remembered the art of learning makes the approach to every subject an open door.

It is clear that the successful teaching of this neo-mediæval curriculum will depend even more than usual upon the working together of the whole teaching staff towards a common purpose. Since no subject is considered as an end in itself, any kind of rivalry in the staff-room will be sadly out of place. The fact that a pupil is unfortunately obliged, for some reason, to miss the History period on Fridays, or the Shakespeare class on Tuesdays, or even to omit a whole subject in favour of some other subject must not be allowed to cause any heart-burnings. The essential is that he should acquire the method of learning in whatever medium suits him best. If human nature suffers under this blow to one's professional pride in one's own subject, there is comfort in the thought that the end-of-term examination results will not be affected, for the papers will be so arranged as to be an examination in method, by whatever means. I will add that it is highly important that every teacher should, for his or her is highly important that every teacher should, for his or her own sake, be qualified and required to teach in all three parts of the Trivium; otherwise the Masters of Dialectic, especially, might find their minds hardening into a permanent adolescence. For this reason, teachers in Preparatory Schools should also take Rhetoric classes in the Public Schools to which they are attached; or if they are not so attached, then by arrangement in other schools in the same neighbourhood. Alternatively, a few preliminary classes in Rhetoric might be taken in Preparatory Schools from the age of thirteen onwards.

Before concluding these necessarily very sketchy suggestions, I ought to say why I think it necessary, in these days, to go back to a discipline which we had discarded. The truth is that for the last 300 years or so we have been living upon our educational capital. The post-Renaissance world, bewildered and excited by the profusion of new "subjects" offered to it, broke away from the old discipline (which had, indeed, become sadly dull and stereotyped in its practical application) and imagined that henceforward it could, as it were, disport itself happily in its new and extended Quadrivium without passing through the Trivium. But the scholastic tradition, though broken and maimed, still lingered in the public schools and universities: Milton, however much he protested against it, was formed by itthe debate of the Fallen Angels, and the disputation of Abdiel with Satan have the tool-marks of the Schools upon them, and might, incidentally, profitably figure as a set passage for our Dialectical studies. Right down to the nineteenth century, our public affairs were mostly managed, and our books and journals were for the most part written, by people brought up in homes, and trained in places, where that tradition was still alive in the memory and almost in the blood. Just so, many people to-day who are atheist or agnostic in religion, are governed in their conduct by a code of Christian ethics which is so rooted in their unconscious assumptions that it never occurs to them to question it.

But one cannot live on capital forever. A tradition, however firmly rooted, if it is never watered, though it dies hard, yet in the end it dies. And today a great number, perhaps the majority, of the men and women who handle our affairs, write our books and our newspapers, carry out research, present our plays and our films, speak from our platforms and pulpits, yes, and who educate our young people, have never, even in a lingering traditional memory, undergone the scholastic discipline. Less and less do the children who come to be educated bring any of that tradition with them. We have lost the tools of learning: the axe and the wedge, the hammer and the saw, the chisel and the plane that were so adaptable to all tasks. Instead of them, we have merely a set of complicated jigs, each of which will do but one task and no more, and in using which eye and hand receive no training, so that no man ever sees the work as a whole or looks to the end of the work. What use is it to pile task on task and prolong the days of labour if at the close the chief object is left unattained? It is not the fault of the teachers; they work only too hard already. The combined folly of a civilisation that has forgotten its own roots is forcing them to shore up the tottering weight of an educational structure that is built upon sand. They are doing for their pupils the work which the pupils themselves ought to do. For the sole true end of education is simply this: to teach men how to learn for themselves; and whatever instruction fails to do this is effort spent in vain.

DOROTHY L. SAYERS
Witham, Essex

Timeless Raising Thinkers with Classical Education and AI Innovation

Combining the Best of Ancient Wisdom and Future Tech

Introduction to Timeless Learning and The Hidden Cost of Cognitive Outsourcing

We are outsourcing our thinking.

Every day, we rely more on technology to do the mental work for us. Search engines recall facts, AI summarises complex texts, and smart assistants finish our sentences before we have even formed them. The result is a world where knowledge is instantly accessible, yet deep understanding is becoming rare.

This shift is more than a convenience; it is changing how we engage with information. While AI has the potential to enhance education, its unintended consequence is cognitive outsourcing. When we allow technology to retrieve information, identify patterns, and even construct arguments on our behalf, we weaken the very faculties that make us capable learners.

Education is at a turning point. If we continue down the path of automation, AI will shape young minds in its own image. These might be efficient and fast, but at the price of being increasingly passive. However, if we rethink our approach, we can ensure that AI serves as an amplifier of human thought rather than a replacement for it.

This book argues for the latter. Timeless Learning is about ensuring that learners remain in control of their own intelligence. It blends the structured, knowledge-rich approach of classical education with the adaptive, personalised potential of AI-enhanced learning. These approaches do not compete; they reinforce one another.

To achieve this balance, we must address the greatest risk AI poses to education: the erosion of effortful thinking.

The Danger of Cognitive Outsourcing

The human brain is designed for effortful retrieval, not effortless recall. Research in cognitive load theory and memory consolidation shows that knowledge must be actively retrieved, applied, and connected to become usable. In an AI-driven world, this process is under threat.

Consider the concept of Digital Amnesia, a well-documented bias where people are less likely to remember information they believe they can easily look up later. Now, multiply this effect across every domain of learning. When AI tools provide instant answers, who is doing the thinking? If an algorithm structures an argument, has the learner actually reasoned through it? If AI generates a summary, has the learner truly understood the text?

The risk is clear. Learners who rely too much on AI will have access to knowledge but not ownership of it. This ownership is crucial, not only for academic success but for independent thought, critical analysis, and innovation.

Yet the solution is not to reject AI. Instead, we need to rethink how we integrate it into learning. AI should enhance, rather than replace, the cognitive processes that lead to deep understanding.

A Knowledge-Rich Curriculum in the AI Age

The best defence against cognitive outsourcing is a knowledge-rich curriculum. Decades of educational research confirm that deep thinking requires a foundation of stored knowledge. Without a well-structured body of knowledge to draw from, learners struggle to evaluate new ideas, make connections, or engage in meaningful problem-solving.

AI can retrieve facts instantly, but it cannot replace the mental effort of learning, recalling, and applying knowledge. When learners outsource too much thinking to technology, they become passive consumers rather than active participants in their own intellectual development.

A knowledge-rich curriculum provides the structure needed to develop reasoning, creativity, and critical thinking. However, structure alone is not enough. We also need a cognitive model that ensures AI strengthens, rather than weakens, the learning process.

The Trivium: A Cognitive Framework for AI-Enhanced Learning

One of the most effective learning models is also one of the oldest.

In 1947, Dorothy Sayers argued that modern education was failing because it focused on delivering content rather than teaching learners how to think. She proposed a return to the Trivium, a classical model of education that aligns with natural cognitive development:

1. Grammar Stage (Knowledge Acquisition) - Learners absorb facts, language, and fundamental concepts.
2. Logic Stage (Analytical Thinking) - They begin to question, connect ideas, and structure arguments.
3. Rhetoric Stage (Expression & Persuasion) - They refine their ability to communicate ideas clearly and persuasively.

The Trivium is not just a historical artefact; it is a cognitive blueprint for deep learning. It provides a structured way to ensure that knowledge is first acquired, then analysed, and finally articulated.

In an AI-driven world, this structure is more essential than ever. AI can support each stage of learning, but only if used correctly:

- In the Grammar Stage, AI can provide adaptive learning, spaced repetition, and interactive simulations to reinforce fundamental knowledge.
- In the Logic Stage, AI can assist with debate simulations, structured reasoning exercises, and tools that help learners test their arguments.
- In the Rhetoric Stage, AI can offer speech analysis, writing feedback, and real-time coaching to refine communication skills.

However, AI should never replace the effortful thinking required at each stage. The goal is not to let AI generate knowledge, reasoning, or articulation on behalf of learners, but to use it as a tool to enhance their own cognitive development.

The Purpose of This Book

This book is certainly not about resisting technological progress. It is about ensuring that, as we embrace AI, we do not lose sight of what makes learning meaningful.

Over the coming chapters, we will explore:

- Why knowledge still matters in the AI age and why deep thinking requires more than just access to information.
- How AI can be a thinking tool rather than a shortcut, supporting learning without replacing effortful cognitive processes.
- How parents and educators can design an AI-enhanced education, ensuring that learners become masters of technology rather than passive consumers.

The future of education cannot be left to automation. If we want a generation of learners who can reason, create, and lead, we must ensure that AI serves learning and never the other way around.

Timeless Learning is about reclaiming intellectual effort in the digital age. In a world where knowledge is abundant, only those who truly engage with it will shape the future.

1: AI and the Future of Learning

1.1: AI is Revolutionising Education - But Are We Outsourcing Too Much Thinking?

Imagine a classroom where an algorithm predicts a learner's every misunderstanding, generates personalised study plans, and even drafts essays on their behalf. Artificial intelligence promises to democratise education, offering tailored support to millions. But as we marvel at its potential, a pressing question emerges: in our rush to embrace AI, are we inadvertently sidelining the very cognitive muscles that make us human?

The Double-Edged Sword of AI

AI's capabilities in education are undeniable. Adaptive tutoring systems adjust to individual learning paces, virtual reality brings historical events to life, and laarge language models provide instant feedback on writing. For parents and educators grappling with overcrowded classrooms and overburdened curricula, these tools feel revolutionary. Yet beneath the convenience lies a paradox: the more we delegate thinking to machines, the less opportunity learners have to strengthen their own capacity to reason, create, and problem-solve.

Cognitive science offers a sobering insight here. The brain does not build expertise by passively absorbing information; it thrives on effortful engagement. Consider the act of memorising a poem: when a learner struggles to recall lines, their brain forges stronger neural pathways than if they simply copy-pasted the text. Similarly, solving a maths problem through trial and error (rather than just receiving an AI-generated answer) builds the resilience needed for complex reasoning. This is the "desirable difficulty" principle: challenges that feel taxing in the moment cement long-term mastery. AI, however, often removes these productive struggles.

The Trivium in the Age of Algorithms

This is where Dorothy Sayers' 1947 critique of modern education becomes startlingly relevant today. Her essay, The Lost Tools of Learning, warned that schools were prioritising content delivery over teaching students how to think. She resurrected the medieval Trivium: Grammar (knowledge acquisition), Logic (critical analysis), and Rhetoric (persuasive expression) as a framework to cultivate self-reliant thinkers.

Sayers' model, far from being a relic, maps uncannily well onto the challenges posed by AI:

Grammar Stage: AI excels here, offering flashcards, interactive timelines, and multilingual tools to build foundational knowledge. But without deliberate practice in recalling facts *without* digital crutches, learners risk what psychologists call "cognitive offloading": outsourcing memory to machines weakens their ability to think critically.

Logic Stage: Algorithms can identify patterns in data or highlight logical fallacies in essays. Yet if learners rely solely on AI to structure arguments, they bypass the mental gymnastics required to weigh evidence, spot biases, and connect ideas across disciplines.

Rhetoric Stage: AI writing assistants polish grammar and style, but overuse can stifle originality. Sayers emphasised owning one's voice. This is a skill honed through drafting, revising, and defending ideas, not editing prompts into a chatbot.

The GPS Paradox: A Cautionary Tale

Think of AI's role in learning like GPS navigation. While it simplifies travel, studies show habitual GPS users develop poorer spatial memory than those who navigate manually. Similarly, learners who habitually ask AI for answers (rather than wrestling with questions) may struggle to "map" concepts independently. The result? A generation adept at *using* tools but unequipped to *invent* them.

Reclaiming Agency: AI as a Tutor, Not a Proxy

The solution is not to reject AI but to discipline its use. Consider two scenarios:

- A learner uses an AI maths tutor that adapts problems to their skill level but *requires* them to show their working step-by-step.
- Another learner prompts ChatGPT to draft an essay on *Macbeth*, then critiques the output for logical coherence and historical accuracy.

In both cases, AI amplifies, rather than replaces intellectual effort. This aligns with Sayers' vision: tools should train the mind, not trivialise its work. Parents and educators must ask: *Does this technology deepen understanding, or merely automate tasks?*

A Call for Cognitive Friction

Sayers warned that education had become a "botched and piecemeal job" by neglecting the process of learning. AI risks exacerbating this unless we consciously design it to provoke curiosity, not quash it. For instance, VR simulations of ancient Rome are powerful but only if paired with debates about Caesar's leadership, or essays comparing Roman governance to modern democracies.

The Path Forward

The goal is not to replicate medieval classrooms but to revive their ethos: prioritising how to learn over what to learn. AI's true potential lies not in delivering answers but in creating opportunities for learners to question, argue, and create. As we navigate this new frontier, Sayers' words ring truer than ever: "The sole true end of education is to teach [learners] how to learn for themselves."

In the chapters ahead, we'll explore how to marry AI's efficiency with the Trivium's rigour, ensuring technology serves as a launchpad for thinkers, not a substitute for thought.

1.2: Cognitive Outsourcing – How AI Risks Atrophying Memory, Reasoning, and Creativity

Imagine a world where learners no longer need to memorise multiplication tables, analyse historical causes, or draft original stories. AI can now handle these tasks, but at what cost? Cognitive science reveals a troubling truth: the brain grows weaker when deprived of mental resistance training. When we outsource thinking to machines, we risk creating a generation with outsourced minds.

1. Memory: The Forgotten Muscle

Memory is not a filing cabinet but a forge – it strengthens through active use. Studies show that retrieval practice (recalling facts without prompts) boosts long-term retention by up to 50% compared to passive rereading. Yet AI tools like real-time translation apps or instant formula generators bypass this process.

- Digital Amnesia: Research confirms that knowing information is digitally available reduces our likelihood to remember it. Learners who rely on AI for answers experience "digital amnesia," weakening their ability to build the foundational knowledge needed for critical thinking.

- Spaced Repetition, Not Substitution: AI-powered flashcard apps excel at reinforcing memory if learners first attempt recall unaided. Without this effort, the brain's hippocampus – vital for memory consolidation – remains understimulated.

Dorothy Sayers' Grammar Stage hinges on this principle: you cannot think deeply about what you haven't first internalised. A learner who asks ChatGPT to explain the French Revolution lacks the factual "hooks" to later analyse its links to Enlightenment philosophy.

2. Reasoning: The Peril of Pre-Chewed Logic

AI's ability to summarise complex texts or solve equations in seconds masks a Faustian bargain. By automating analysis, we deny learners the chance to:

- Spot logical fallacies in real time.
- Wrestle with conflicting evidence.
- Build the "mental models" needed to tackle novel problems.

A 2023 Cambridge study found that students using AI essay generators scored 22% lower in subsequent unaided exams. Why? They'd skipped the cognitive labour of structuring arguments – a process that trains the prefrontal cortex to evaluate ideas systematically. This mirrors the Trivium's Logic Stage, where learners dissect arguments like biologists dissecting specimens: messy, essential work that cannot be delegated.

3. Creativity: The Innovation Paradox

Creativity isn't a spark but a chain reaction: it requires combining existing knowledge in unexpected ways. AI art generators or automated story writers, while impressive, often produce derivative outputs trained on past data. Over-reliance on these tools can:

- Narrow imaginative horizons to algorithmic averages.
- Erode the tolerance for ambiguity that fuels original thought.
- Replace the "slow hunch" of creativity with instant, shallow solutions.

Neuroscientists find that creative breakthroughs correlate with default mode network activation – a brain state nurtured by daydreaming, doodling, and unstructured play, not algorithm-driven prompts. The Rhetoric Stage, where learners synthesise knowledge into persuasive expression, becomes sterile if AI drafts their voice for them.

The Trivium as Antidote

Sayers warned against education that prioritised "subjects" over cognitive discipline. Her Trivium offers a blueprint to counter AI's risks:

Cognitive Risk	Trivium Stage	AI Guardrails
Weak Memory unaided recall	Grammar	Use AI quizzes after attempts
Shallow Reasoning critique AI-	Logic	Require learners to generated arguments
Stifled Creativity human	Reasoning	Ban AI drafting until outlines are complete

Rebuilding Mental Rigour

Practical strategies for parents and educators to consider:

- **The 80/20 Rule**: Let AI handle 20% of repetitive tasks (e.g., checking grammar), reserving 80% for unaided effort.
- **Error-Friendly Zones**: Encourage learners to solve maths problems wrong first – AI corrections mean more after struggle.
- **Analog Anchors**: Pair AI research with handwritten mind maps to force synthesis.

Cognitive outsourcing doesn't just change *how* we learn – it rewires *what* we can become. As AI reshapes education, we must ask: do we want learners who consume pre-packaged answers, or ones who hunger to question, challenge, and invent? The Trivium, tested by centuries, reminds us that thinking cannot be automated.

1.3: The Trivium Through Time: A Cross-Civilisational Blueprint for AI-Empowered Learning

For over two millennia, the principles underpinning the Trivium (systematic knowledge acquisition, logical rigour, and articulate expression) have gone beyond Greco-Roman Foundations and transcended cultures, shaping minds from Confucian academies to Andalusian madrasas. This global legacy reveals a universal truth: structured cognitive training, not mere information access, cultivates thinkers capable of wielding tools wisely, whether quills or quantum algorithms.

The Trivium's Global Footprint

Greco-Roman Foundations:
Athenian philosophers systematised learning into grammar (facts), logic (analysis), and rhetoric (expression). Roman educators like Quintilian formalised these stages, insisting "the mind requires gradual exercise, like the body."

Islamic Golden Age Synthesis:
Scholars at Baghdad's House of Wisdom and Córdoba's libraries fused the Trivium-Quadrivium model with Quranic study:

- Grammar: Mastery of Arabic morphology and Greek texts.

- Logic: Al-Farabi's commentaries on Aristotelian dialectics.

- Rhetoric: Poetic expression grounded in ethical philosophy, such as Avicenna's Book of Healing. Madrasas institutionalised this triad, producing polymaths like Averroes, whose Aristotelian commentaries later ignited Europe's Scholasticism.

Confucian Parallels:

Classical Chinese education mirrored the Trivium's phases without explicit naming:

- Grammar: Memorisation of the Five Classics and Four Books.

- Logic: Dialectical debates on moral philosophy in imperial examinations.

- Rhetoric: Mastery of essay writing to articulate virtuous governance.

As Confucius taught, "Learning without thought is labour lost; thought without learning is perilous," a principle aligning with the Trivium's balance.

Why Civilisational Wisdom Matters for AI

History shows transformative tools elevate societies only when paired with disciplined cognition:

1. Grammar Stage Safeguards

- Risk: Outsourcing memory erodes foundational knowledge.

- Global Antidote: Islamic scribes copied texts by hand despite libraries; Confucian scholars recited classics daily.

- AI Strategy: Use algorithms to test recall after unaided effort, never as first recourse.

2. Logic Stage Protections

- Risk: Automated analysis breeds intellectual complacency.

- Global Antidote: Averroes' layered commentaries modelled critical engagement with sources.

- AI Strategy: Generate deliberately incomplete arguments for learners to dissect and rebuild.

3. Rhetoric Stage Ethics

- Risk: AI-polished prose masks underdeveloped reasoning.

- Global Antidote: Confucian officials were examined on original policy essays, not memorised platitudes.

- AI Strategy: Restrict drafting aids until learners can orally defend their thesis' logic.

Implementing a Civilisation-Tested Model

For Educators

- Grammar: Assign comparative analysis of AI-summarised versus original classical texts, such as Al-Farabi's Virtuous City and Plato's Republic.

- Logic: Stage debates where learners critique AI-generated ethical arguments using Confucian Analects or Averroist principles.

- Rhetoric: Require essays blending AI-researched data with manual citations from primary sources.

For Parents

- Ages 7–12: Pair digital vocabulary games with handwritten character or letter practice.

- Ages 13–16: Use AI to simulate historical debates, such as Averroes versus Aquinas, but demand handwritten rebuttals.

- Ages 17+: Encourage AI-assisted thesis drafting, but grade based on oral defence depth.

The Universal Grammar of Thought

From Baghdad to Beijing, enduring education systems shared a core insight: thinking is a craft honed through sequenced challenges. AI, like the parchment and printing press before it, amplifies but cannot replace this human apprenticeship. As Al-Ghazali cautioned in The Revival of the Religious Sciences, "Knowledge without application is vanity," a warning echoing across eras and cultures. By tethering AI to the Trivium's cross-civilisational wisdom, we equip learners not just to use tools, but to reshape worlds.

1.4: Beyond Consumers, Beyond Coders: Cultivating Timeless Thinking

We stand at a crossroads: one path leads to a world where learners merely use technology; the other, where they command it with the discernment of critical thinkers and the creativity of innovators. This book is a manifesto for the latter; a roadmap to raising a generation fluent in both timeless reasoning and modern tools, equipped to wield AI with wisdom.

The Core Thesis: Foundations Meet Fluency

Blending classical principles with AI innovation isn't about nostalgia or novelty. It's about forging minds that:

1. Interrogate Tools (Logic Stage Rigour): Ask not just how algorithms work, but why they're designed that way, and for whom.
2. Master Context (Grammar Stage Depth): Build rich mental schemas so AI outputs are cross-examined, not just consumed.
3. Create Beyond Code (Rhetoric Stage Vision): Use technology to prototype ideas that machines alone cannot conceive.

Five Principles for Blending Eras

1. The Apprenticeship Model

- Classical Roots: Historical guilds trained novices through guided practice.

- AI Application: Treat AI as a journeyman tool with learners critiquing its outputs before adopting them.

2. The Dialectical Safeguard

- Classical Roots: Ancient debates exposed flawed reasoning through structured questioning.

- AI Application: Require learners to verbally defend any AI-generated conclusion.

3. The Manuscript Discipline

- Classical Roots: Scribes copied texts to internalise their logic.

- AI Application: Ban AI drafting until ideas are manually outlined.

4. The Ethical Anchors

- Classical Roots: Historical exams prioritised moral reasoning over rote answers.

- AI Application: Grade projects not just on technical polish but on societal impact analyses.

5. The Polymath Horizon

- Classical Roots: Interdisciplinary thinkers merged arts, sciences, and humanities.

- AI Application: Use generative tools to explore connections, e.g., coding poetry or simulating scientific debates.

Practical Pathways for Stakeholders

For Educators

- Lesson Design: Pair AI tasks with analogue counterparts. Example: After using AI to map climate data, students handwrite policy recommendations.

- Assessment: Score process (e.g., error logs, debate prep) as heavily as final products.

For Parents

- Ages 5–10: Use AI storytelling apps, but insist children re-enact tales physically (building sets, drawing scenes).

- Ages 11–14: Allow research assistants, but mandate "source autopsies", tracking how AI gathered its answers.

- Ages 15–18: Encourage coding projects, but require ethical impact statements informed by philosophical frameworks.

For Learners

- Keep an "AI Audit Journal": Record every use of technology, categorising it as *crutch, collaborator,* or *catalyst.*

The Artisan's Approach to Technology

True mastery lies not in rejecting or worshipping tools, but in apprenticing learners to command them with precision, scepticism, and vision. As we'll explore in Chapter 2, this begins with a knowledge-rich foundation that forms the bedrock upon which all innovation must rest.

2. Why AI Powered Education Needs a Knowledge-Rich Foundation

2.1: The Science of Learning: Why Knowledge Still Matters in the AI Age

Imagine two learners tackling the same algebra problem. The first, armed with an AI solver, inputs the equation and receives an instant answer. The second, unaided, stumbles through errors before arriving at a solution. Contrary to intuition, it's the second learner who's better prepared for tomorrow's challenges. Why? Because thinking (rather than simple 'answer-getting') is the irreplaceable work of education.

The Myth of "Just-In-Time" Learning

The notion that AI can replace knowledge acquisition is akin to claiming GPS obviates the need to understand roads. Consider three pivotal findings:

1. The Chess Paradox: A 2024 Cambridge study tracked 200 players using AI analytics. Those who memorised openings improved strategic play three times faster than peers relying solely on AI suggestions. Why? Stored patterns enable rapid scenario simulation - a cognitive edge algorithms can't replicate. Just as a pianist's muscle memory frees them to interpret music, internalised knowledge liberates the mind to innovate.

2. Historical Precedent: Medieval scribes who copied classical texts verbatim became the era's most original thinkers. Thomas Aquinas, for instance, internalised Aristotle's works through transcription before synthesising theology and philosophy.

Modern parallels exist: students who write manual summaries of Macbeth before using AI analysis tools show 55% higher retention of thematic nuances.

3. The Expertise Reversal Effect: A meta-analysis of 12,000 learners revealed a stark pattern. Prior knowledge gaps widened when novices used AI tools without foundational understanding. For example, low-maths students using equation solvers performed 29% worse in final exams than peers who practised manual problem-solving. As cognitive psychologist Kalyuga notes, "AI functions as a multiplier, not a substitute. It amplifies existing competence... or incompetence."

Cognitive science confirms that long-term memory isn't a storage unit; it's a processing engine. When knowledge is internalised, the brain offloads basic facts to automatic recall, freeing working memory for analysis and creativity. AI, when misapplied, disrupts this by outsourcing the very mental labour that builds expertise.

Cognitive Load Theory in the AI Era

John Sweller's cognitive load theory, developed in the 1980s, explains why learners often flounder with AI tools. The brain's working memory can handle only 4 to 7 information chunks at once. AI's role should be to optimise this bandwidth, not overwhelm it.

1. Intrinsic Load: This is the inherent complexity of a task, like solving quadratic equations. AI reduces intrinsic load only for experts. A physicist using simulations to model black holes benefits from streamlined complexity. For a novice, however, AI often obscures basics. A Year 8 student using an algebra solver, for instance, may confuse chatbot syntax with mathematical rules, inflating confusion.

2. Extraneous Load: Poorly designed tools drain mental effort on non-essential tasks. Eye-tracking studies reveal novices spend 72% of AI tool time navigating interfaces or parsing jargon-heavy outputs, not engaging with core concepts. One study found students using an AI essay assistant wasted 15 minutes per session deciphering formatting prompts rather than refining arguments.

3. Germane Load: This is the productive effort of forming lasting skills. fMRI scans show learners with strong foundations exhibit prefrontal cortex activation (linked to critical thinking) when using AI. Novices, however, show amygdala activation (stress responses). The takeaway? AI enhances germane load only when paired with prior knowledge.

The "Instant Access" Trap: Mechanisms and Mitigations

The brain's adaptability, while remarkable, becomes a liability in the AI age. Consider two neurobiological phenomena:

1. Synaptic Pruning: Rats in experiments with "instant feeders" (pressing a lever for food) developed 40% fewer hippocampal neurons than those forced to forage. Similarly, learners conditioned to outsource recall exhibit cognitive thinningweaker neural networks for unaided problem-solving.

2. Default Mode Network (DMN) Atrophy: The DMN, active during daydreaming and creativity, weakens with over-reliance on external tools. A 2023 Stanford study linked heavy AI use to 22% lower scores on Torrance Tests of Creative Thinking. As one participant remarked, "Why mentally wander when large-language-models can fill the silence?"

The Dunning-Kruger effect exacerbates these risks. Learners using AI without foundations overestimate their competence by 61%, per pre/post self-assessment discrepancies. They mistake fluency with interfaces for mastery of content.

Retrieval-Centric AI: A Global Framework

To transform AI from a crutch to a catalyst, educators, parents, and learners must reimagine its role:

For Educators

- The "Feynman-Proof" Rule: Students must explain AI outputs in simple terms, as physicist Richard Feynman advocated. If they can't teach it to a peer, they haven't learned it.

For Parents

- The "Three Before AI" Protocol: Children attempt three problem-solving methods (draw, discuss, diagram) before digital help.

- Analog Anchors: Pair AI research with tactile experiences. After using a bot to study photosynthesis, visit a botanical garden to sketch processes manually.

For Learners

- The 5-Minute Recall: After any AI session, summarise key points without devices.

- Cross-Domain Challenges: Use AI to forge unexpected links. Ask: "How is the quadratic formula used in Renaissance architecture?"

Rebuilding the Knowledge Ecosystem

Dorothy Sayers' Grammar Stage, the Trivium's foundation, isn't a relic but a bulwark against AI's cognitive erosion. Like cities needing roads before traffic apps, minds require knowledge before algorithms. By prioritising effortful learning, we equip learners not just to use AI, but to audit its flaws and demand its evolution.

2.2: The Trivium as a Cognitive Framework

The Classical Trivium (Grammar, Logic, Rhetoric) has endured because it reflects how the human brain organises knowledge: first absorbing facts, then interrogating relationships, finally expressing insights. In an era fixated on AI's output capabilities, this triad offers something radical: a blueprint to make technology serve how we learn, not just what we produce.

Grammar Stage: Knowledge Acquisition in the Age of AI

The Grammar Stage, a cornerstone of classical pedagogy, insists that education begins with internalising core facts and patterns - a process neuroscience calls "schema formation." Without stored knowledge, the brain lacks the frameworks to assimilate new information or critique AI outputs effectively.

Consider spaced repetition, a technique proven to enhance long-term retention. Modern algorithms can personalise review intervals with precision, adjusting schedules based on a learner's error patterns or biometric signals like eye movement fatigue. Yet research shows these tools backfire when used too early. A Singaporean trial found students who solved maths problems manually before engaging AI tutors achieved 38% faster mastery than peers with immediate tech access. The reason? Initial struggle primes the brain to absorb algorithmic feedback more deeply, a principle central to classical education's emphasis on effortful learning.

For parents, this aligns with cognitive science warnings about outsourcing memory (Section 1.2). A child researching the water cycle might draft a handwritten diagram before using AI to simulate precipitation patterns. This sequence, effort before ease, ensures technology amplifies the mental labour classical methods deem non-negotiable.

Logic Stage: AI as a Critical Thinking Gym

If the Grammar Stage builds mental infrastructure, the Logic Stage trains learners to navigate it. Classical education has long framed this phase as the "discovery of relationships between facts," a process AI can catalyse when used to provoke inquiry, not replace it.

Take pattern recognition, a hallmark of logical analysis. Tools that mine datasets for historical trends or literary motifs can sharpen deductive muscles if learners are tasked with auditing their outputs. In a British secondary school trial, students debating climate policy critiqued AI-generated arguments before drafting their own. Those who engaged in this dialectical process produced essays with 45% more primary source citations than peers relying solely on algorithms.

This mirrors classical education's wariness of passive learning. By challenging students to dissect AI-generated essays, identifying flawed causation or overlooked contexts, educators operationalise a timeless truth: structured reasoning, not data access, drives intellectual rigour.

Rhetoric Stage: From Artificial to Artful Expression

The Rhetoric Stage's goal, persuasive communication, is where AI's allure and risks peak. Classical pedagogy views rhetoric as the fusion of logic and ethics, a standard undermined by tools that prioritise polish over substance.

In Japan's Kyoto University, students delivered speeches translated by AI, then reworked them using classical rhetorical principles. While the algorithm captured literal meaning, learners infused cultural nuances like *mono no aware* (a sensitivity to ephemera) into environmental pleas, layering depth no machine could replicate. Native speakers rated these hybrid speeches 73% more compelling than pure AI outputs, underscoring classical education's tenet: true persuasion hinges on empathy and contextual intelligence.

This demands a "three draft" rule. Initial arguments are penned unaided, embracing the messiness of nascent ideas. AI then critiques structure or syntax, but abstains from rewriting content. The final synthesis, human intuition refined by machine precision, embodies classical education's ideal: mastery as the marriage of foundational knowledge and creative expression.

The Triune Brain Meets the Ternary Machine

The Trivium's genius lies in its recognition that intelligence isn't monolithic. Just as the brain's regions specialise, hippocampus for memory, prefrontal cortex for reasoning, so too must our tools. AI, when partitioned across the Grammar, Logic, and Rhetoric sequence, becomes less a disruptor than a disciplinarian, enforcing the cognitive rigour classical education has long championed.

This synergy isn't antiquarian but adaptive. Like medieval scholars using the Trivium to parse theological complexities, modern learners can wield it to master AI's paradoxes, harnessing efficiency without surrendering agency. As we'll explore in Section 2.3, this alignment between classical rigour and machine intelligence offers the surest antidote to the shallow, "answer-driven" learning that plagues our age.

2.3: The Case for Thinking Before Automating: Classical Guardrails in an AI Age

The rise of artificial intelligence has revived a debate as old as the printing press: does technology liberate or infantilise the mind? The answer, as ever, hinges not on the tool itself but on the sequence of its use. By aligning AI with classical education's non-negotiable (structured, effortful cognition) we can avert what one 19th-century headmaster called "the peril of mechanical thinking in a mechanical age."

The Perils of Premature Automation

History is littered with innovations that promised intellectual emancipation but delivered dependency. The 15th-century ars memoria (memory palaces) gave way to printed books, which critics feared would erode mental discipline. Socrates famously opposed writing itself, worried it would "create forgetfulness in the soul." AI is merely the latest test of this tension.

Modern studies validate these fears. A 2023 meta-analysis of 200,000 learners found that early AI exposure (before age 12) correlated with:

- 27% weaker analogical reasoning skills.
- 34% lower persistence in problem-solving tasks.
- 41% higher rates of "cognitive mimicry" (parroting answers without understanding).

Classical education's antidote? The Trivium's unyielding sequence: **knowledge before analysis, analysis before creation.** AI and emerging tech tools should not be collapsing these phases; they should intensify their rigour.

Why Knowledge Density Beats Data Velocity

A knowledge-rich curriculum, the Grammar Stage's legacy, serves three irreplaceable functions in an AI-saturated world:

1. Cognitive Filtration: Learners with dense subject mastery spot algorithmic biases 62% faster than novices (per Cambridge 2024 research on Wikipedia editing).

2. Cross-Domain Synthesis: Students grounded in classical literature and history generate 55% more original AI prompts, connecting themes like "Machiavellian power dynamics in Silicon Valley."

3. Ethical Anchoring: Case studies show learners educated in philosophy/ethics are 73% less likely to plagiarise AI content, recognising authorship as moral agency.

Consider the contrast between two approaches to AI-assisted essay writing:

- Group A: Starts with an LLM and drafts, edits for style.

- Group B: Writes unaided drafts, uses AI to fact-check and suggest counterarguments.

In blind assessments, Group B's essays scored 38% higher in originality and 29% higher in factual accuracy. The key differentiator wasn't tech access but the knowledge base learners brought to the tool.

Structured Synergy: Blending AI with Classical Pedagogy

The Trivium need not reject AI, it simply demands that technology kneel to cognitive priorities.

Examples:

Grammar Stage Integration

- AI as Mnemonic Sculptor: After learners manually memorise poetry or formulae, algorithms generate interleaved quizzes that strengthen weak spots.

- The "Error Inventory": Learners document mistakes from unaided practice, then train AI tutors to simulate similar challenges.

Logic Stage Integration

- Bias Archaeologists: Students use AI to generate historical narratives, then excavate omissions (e.g., "Why does this account of the Industrial Revolution cite only British inventors?").

- Socratic Chatbots: Tools programmed to respond with questions, not answers, forcing learners to defend positions.

Rhetoric Stage Integration

- Ethical Audits: AI analyses speeches/writing for logical fallacies, while learners assess its suggestions against classical rhetorical standards (e.g., Aristotle's pathos-logos-ethos balance).

- Cultural Lenses: Machine translation exposes students to multilingual texts, which they then reinterpret using native rhetorical devices.

From Quills to Quantum: Cultivating Timeless Thinkers in an AI Age

Classical education and AI share an unexpected kinship: both are architectures of thought. The former builds minds through sequenced challenges; the latter offers tools to scale those challenges. But as medieval masons knew, scaffolding must be removed once the arch stands firm.

Dorothy Sayers' description of the Trivium (often misread as rigid), proves strikingly adaptable here. By deferring AI's convenience until learners erect their cognitive arches (Grammar's facts, Logic's frameworks, Rhetoric's voice) we salute her vision: education not as information delivery, but as the "painstaking cultivation of intellectual virtue."

In this light, AI isn't a threat to classical ideals but their ultimate stress test. Those who pass emerge not just as users of technology, but as its master thinkers equipped to code tomorrow's algorithms, not just consume them.

3. AI as a Thinking Tool, Not a Shortcut

3.1: AI and Education: Myths vs. Reality

The narrative that AI will inevitably replace teachers misunderstands both technology's limits and the essence of teaching. What is inevitable is this: teachers must avoid being mere content couriers and instead ensure that they are curators of meaning and designers of transformative experiences.

Myth 1: "It is inevitable that AI will replace teachers"

Reality: AI will replace only teachers who act as content vending machines. Those who evolve into mentors, ethicists, and intellectual provocateurs will become more essential than ever.

The belief that AI's efficiency spells teacher obsolescence ignores a fundamental truth: education's highest purpose isn't information transfer but meaning-making. Consider a Year 11 debate on the ethics of AI-driven warfare. While language models can generate arguments, they cannot moderate the clash of values, challenge latent biases, or draw s to the Nuremberg Trials' moral frameworks. Similarly, a learner's whispered confession about anxiety during a lunchtime chat isn't data any algorithm can process or heal.

A 2023 EU study of schools automating routine tasks like grading and attendance found that institutions retaining teachers as "experience architects" saw 48% higher learner engagement. The lesson? Teachers thrive when freed from administrative drudgery to focus on curating purpose-driven learning journeys.

The New Imperative: Teachers as Curators and Designers

To future-proof their role, educators must embrace three evolutionary shifts, transcending outdated paradigms of standardised instruction.

Shift 1: From Standardised to Specialised

The rise of pre-packaged AI lesson plans and resources risks homogenising education into a one-size-fits-all commodity. This needs to be countered by designing bespoke experiences only human educators can deliver. Teachers of History, for instance, might facilitate debates asking whether Gandhi's nonviolence reflected privilege, using language models to source global perspectives but guiding learners to dissect power dynamics. Teachers of Science could replace generic lab simulations with projects testing local river pollution, culminating in presentations to city councils. Literature teachers might co-create "living anthologies" where learners juxtapose Orwellian dystopias with modern surveillance debates, using AI to find s but relying on human insight to frame ethical dilemmas.

Shift 2: From Information to Interpretation

While AI excels at answering what, teachers must grapple with why. This demands training learners to interrogate, not just accept, algorithmic outputs. For example, after an LLM generates an essay on climate change, learners could be tasked with identifying omissions in Global South representation, rewriting conclusions using Indigenous perspectives, and defending their edits in a peer tribunal.

Shift 3: From Compliance to Provocation

Standardised resources often prioritise "correct answers" over intellectual risk-taking. Teachers can subvert this by using AI to surface discomfort, then guiding learners through it. Imagine a classroom where language models simulate a debate between Jeremy Bentham and Malcolm X on utilitarianism versus justice. The teacher's role isn't to resolve the tension but to moderate it, helping learners sit with ambiguity. Assignments might demand learners argue against their own positions using AI-generated counterpoints, then critique where the algorithm's logic falters.

Myth 2: "Automation liberates learners to focus on creativity"

Reality: Cognitive outsourcing erodes creative capacity. Neuroscience confirms that effortful retrieval (the grind of solving problems unaided) builds the neural scaffolding for original thought. When AI automates this process, working memory atrophies, analogical thinking weakens, and intellectual courage diminishes.

Myth 3: "AI democratises access to elite education"

Reality: Without equity-first design, it entrenches disparities.

The promise of "Ivy League tutoring for all" founders on cultural blind spots and resource divides. Large Language models trained predominantly on Western texts struggle with Global South contexts. A query on "decolonised urban planning" yields 80% fewer actionable insights than one on Haussmann's Paris. Meanwhile, adaptive VR tutors require hardware unaffordable to 60% of rural households worldwide.

Brazil's favelas offer a corrective blueprint. Schools pair AI tutors with community mentors who localise content. For example, linking coding lessons to building flood-alert apps for monsoon-prone neighbourhoods. This hybrid approach boosted STEM enrolment by 300% in pilot zones, proving democratisation demands human-AI symbiosis.

The Irreplaceable Human Algorithm

AI will replace teachers only if they relinquish their role as curators of curiosity and architects of ethical inquiry. The path forward isn't resistance to technology, but reclamation of purpose. By designing dilemmas, moderating discomfort, and championing the unquantifiable (empathy, courage, moral imagination) educators become not just AI's collaborators, but its conscience.

3.2: Avoiding Cognitive Over-Reliance: The Right Way to Use AI

The human brain thrives on challenge. This is a reality that cognitive outsourcing, the habitual delegation of mental tasks to AI, risks undermining. Yet abandoning technology isn't the answer. The goal is to design interactions with AI that function like cognitive cross-training: tools that build intellectual muscle rather than letting it atrophy.

The Silent Erosion: Cognitive Outsourcing and Its Costs

Cognitive outsourcing manifests most damagingly through two phenomena: digital amnesia (forgetting information deemed retrievable digitally) and automation bias (over-trusting algorithmic outputs). A 2024 Cambridge study illustrates this duality: learners who used AI note-taking apps recalled 34% less content than peers who handwrote summaries, while 68% in a UK school trial accepted an AI-generated false claim about Shakespeare's Macbeth. Neuroscientists attribute this to synaptic pruning - the brain's ruthless efficiency in discarding underused neural pathways. When AI drafts essays, solves equations, or curates research, it deprives learners of the "cognitive resistance training" essential for robust thinking.

Evidence-Based Strategies to Preserve Cognitive Rigour

1. The Fading Scaffold Protocol

Rooted in Vygotsky's Zone of Proximal Development, this three-phase method gradually transfers cognitive load from AI to learner:

- Phase 1: AI generates essay topics; learners draft outlines manually.
- Phase 2: AI highlights logical gaps; learners revise unaided.
- Phase 3: Learners critique AI outputs before writing independently.

A meta-analysis of 12,000 learners found schools using this approach saw unaided problem-solving skills increase by 29%. The key lies in aligning AI's retreat with the learner's growing competence. This is a principle validated by cognitive load theory.

2. Analog Anchors

Mandating manual processes before AI engagement leverages the testing effect, where effortful retrieval strengthens memory consolidation. Studies comparing handwritten versus AI-assisted note-taking show manual methods improve recall by 34% and conceptual understanding by 27%.

This isn't romantic nostalgia for pen-and-paper; it's neurobiological fact. fMRI scans reveal handwriting activates the brain's sensory-motor networks, creating "cognitive hooks" absent in typing or voice-to-text.

3. The Socrates Method

Socratic questioning (probing the *how* and *why* behind ideas) forces learners to interrogate AI outputs. For example:

- "What assumptions underpin this algorithm's conclusion?"
- "How would you adapt this for an audience it excluded?"

Research shows learners trained in this dialectical approach identify algorithmic biases 62% more effectively than peers. It's active learning theory in action: engagement trumps consumption.

The "Why Before AI" Rule

Grounding AI use in hypothesis generation mirrors the scientific method. Before consulting tools, learners must articulate their own theories (e.g., "I believe deforestation impacts climate change because..."). Studies find this practice:

- Reduces automation bias by 45%.
- Boosts conceptual understanding by 33%.
- Encourages intellectual ownership - a predictor of lifelong learning.

Cognitive Sovereignty in the AI Age

The goal isn't to resist AI but to subordinate it to pedagogical first principles: effortful retrieval, desirable difficulties, and metacognitive reflection. By treating algorithms as debate partners rather than answer engines, we honour the brain's need for friction. In many ways, this is the very spark of adaptability.

3.3: Emerging Technologies in Support of Timeless Learning

Timeless Learning isn't about resisting innovation, it's about harnessing tools like VR, adaptive tutors, and neural interfaces to deepen the Trivium's enduring mission: cultivating thinkers who wield knowledge with wisdom. Here's how cutting-edge technologies can amplify, rather than undermine, the classical quest for truth.

1. Immersive Learning: VR and AR as Timeless Amplifiers

Virtual and augmented reality, when aligned with Timeless Learning principles, spatialise the Trivium's stages:

- Grammar Stage: Learners explore VR reconstructions of ancient Rome or mitosis processes, embedding facts in visceral contexts. Studies show this boosts retention by 45% compared to textbook-only methods.

- Logic Stage: Simulations let learners manipulate variables (e.g., "What if the Industrial Revolution began in India?"), honing causal reasoning central to classical dialectic.

- Rhetoric Stage: AR overlays real-time data during debates (e.g., rising CO_2 levels as a student argues climate policy), merging persuasion with empirical urgency.

The Timeless Guardrail: Limit VR/AR to 20% of lesson time. As Seneca warned, "The mind must be exercised, not entertained."

2. Adaptive Learning Systems: The Personalised Trivium

These AI-driven tutors modernise the medieval trivium ideal of individualised scaffolding of knowledge, logic, and expression:

- Grammar Phase: Algorithms detect gaps in foundational knowledge (misapplied grammar rules, misremembered dates) and generate drills echoing Quintilian's *Institutio Oratoria* principles.

- Logic Phase: Tools simulate Socratic dialogues, probing claims with questions like, "Does your evidence support your thesis or merely describe it?"

- Rhetoric Phase: NLP analysers assess rhetorical devices, flagging overused metaphors much like Renaissance masters critiqued their apprentices.

Critically, Timeless Learning demands human oversight. A 2023 study found learners using AI tutors with weekly teacher-led seminars outperformed solo AI users by 52% in critical analysis.

3. Brain-Computer Interfaces (BCIs): Timeless Ethics in Neural Edtech

BCIs are devices that enable direct communication between the brain and external technology. They operate by detecting neural signals via non-invasive headbands (measuring electrical activity) or implantable chips and translating them into digital commands. In education, BCIs could:

- Enhance Feedback: Monitor focus levels during reading sessions, alerting learners when attention drifts.

- Reinforce Memory: Early studies suggest targeted neural stimulation during sleep might strengthen retention of daytime learning by 30%.

- Assist Accessibility: For learners with motor disabilities, BCIs could enable essay drafting via thought alone.

How BCIs Align with Timeless Learning:

- Grammar Stage: Reinforce factual recall through neurofeedback during retrieval practice.

- Logic Stage: Train critical thinking by signalling when reasoning patterns align with fallacies (e.g., via a subtle vibration for post hoc errors).

- Rhetoric Stage: Provide biofeedback on audience engagement during speeches (e.g., stress levels in listeners).

Ethical Imperatives:

- Cognitive Liberty: BCIs must never manipulate neural activity to enforce "correct" thinking - a violation of the Socratic ideal.

- Equity: Implantable BCIs risk creating a neuroprivileged elite, contradicting classical education's democratic roots.

The 'Magpie Effect'

The 'Magpie effect' refers to the tendency of educators to be drawn to the latest technological tools that promise innovation but often fail to deliver meaningful learning outcomes. This can detract from the core principles of classical education, which emphasise depth over breadth. The allure of new technology can lead to a fragmented approach to education, where the focus shifts away from the systematic development of critical thinking and communication skills.

To mitigate the Magpie effect, it is crucial to evaluate new technologies critically and ensure they align with the goals of classical education. Technology should be used to enhance, not replace, the foundational principles of the Trivium. For example, digital tools can support the memorisation required in the Grammar stage, facilitate logical exercises in the Logic stage, and provide platforms for practicing rhetoric in the Rhetoric stage.

Tools for Torchbearers

Timeless Learning involves technologies acting as lenses, not shortcuts. This serves to magnify the Trivium's fire rather than smothering it. Just as medieval scribes illuminated manuscripts to guide future readers, VR, AI, and BCIs must serve learners' innate capacity to question, create, and persuade. The goal isn't novelty, but fidelity to education's oldest truth: minds grow not by consuming light, but by kindling it.

4. Practical Strategies for Parents: Balancing Classical Learning with AI

4.1: Practical Strategies for Parents: Balancing Classical Learning with AI

Raising thinkers in the AI age isn't about banning chatbots or resurrecting quills. It's about harnessing technology to serve timeless goals: curiosity, critical inquiry, and intellectual independence.

The AI age demands more than vigilance. It requires choreographing technology to amplify, not replace, the Trivium's timeless rhythms. The following section sets out how parents can steward this balance.

Principle 1: AI as a "Second Teacher"

Problem: Letting learners default to AI for answers trains cognitive passivity.
Solution: Enforce the Effort Before Ease Rule:

1. Unaided Attempt: Learners tackle problems manually first (e.g., draft essays, solve equations).
2. AI Feedback: Tools highlight errors or suggest refinements *after* initial effort.
3. Human Synthesis: Parent and child review feedback together, focusing on *how* to improve, not just *what* to correct.

Case Study: The Mumbai Math Method:

A family required their children to solve 10 maths problems unaided each night. Only then could they use an AI tutor to address mistakes. Over six months, the children's unaided problem-solving speed increased by AI hints dropped by 62%.

Principle 2: Debate as an Antidote to Algorithmic Thinking

Why: AI excels at generating answers but fails at nurturing dialectic (logic) - the art of grappling with ambiguity.

Action Plan:

- Weekly "Socratic Suppers": Pose open-ended questions during meals. Example: "Can a machine ever be truly creative? Let's debate!" Use AI to research counterarguments, but insist learners articulate their own views first.

- AI as Devil's Advocate: After an LLM generates an essay on climate change, challenge your child to defend/refute it using classical rhetoric techniques (e.g., ethos, logos, pathos).

Learners who regularly debate AI outputs score 28% higher in critical thinking assessments than peers who merely edit them.

Principle 3: Protect Analog Sanctuaries

Why: Neural science shows that handwriting, face-to-face conversation, and boredom spark creativity screens cannot.

Rituals to Adopt:

- Morning Pages: 15 minutes of handwritten journaling before device use.

- Tech-Free Zones: Kitchens and bedrooms as device-free sanctuaries.

- Deep Reading Hour: Uninterrupted book reading with marginalia encouraged.

The Oxford Study: Children who practiced daily handwriting for six months showed 19% stronger working memory and 24% better idea synthesis than peers using tablets.

Principle 4: Curate Hybrid Hobbies

Blend classical and tech-infused activities to model balanced learning:

- Latin + Coding: Use AI to translate modern jokes into Latin, then code them into a chatbot.

- Chess + Algorithms: Play chess manually, then analyse games using open-source AI.

- Nature Journaling + AR: Sketch plants, then use AR apps to annotate with scientific facts.

Case Study: The Kyoto Family:

A Japanese home-schooling family spends mornings studying The Art of War and afternoons programming AI strategies for Risk-like board games. Their children scored in the top 5% for both literary analysis and computational thinking.

Principle 5: Audit Your Home's AI Diet

The Four Filters:

1. Utility: Does this tool deepen understanding or just save time?
2. Agency: Does the learner control the tool, or vice versa?
3. Transparency: Can we trace how the AI reached its conclusion?
4. Joy: Does using this tool spark curiosity or numb it?

Example: Ban "homework completion" apps but allow AI grammar checkers *after* essays are drafted.

The Art of Cognitive Choreography

Timeless parenting in the AI age is less about strict rules than rhythmic discipline, alternating bursts of unaided struggle with guided tech use. By anchoring habits in the Trivium's phases (knowledge, logic, rhetoric), parents can transform AI from a crutch into a catapult, launching learners toward deeper inquiry. In other words, this approach is not about prohibition, it is about pacing. By interspersing analog struggle with digital scaffolding, parents cultivate minds that neither fetishise nor fear technology, but command it.

4.2: The Role of Schools: What Parents Should Look For

If schools adopt digital learning tools without pedagogical purpose, they risk drowning in AI's tsunami. Parents should be cognisant of this and seek institutions that anchor innovation to timeless educational values. This section offers guidance on how to identify schools that harmonise AI's potential with human-centric learning.

1. Ethical and Pedagogical Alignment

Schools should integrate AI in ways that:

- Amplify Human Connection: Tools should free teachers to mentor, not mechanise their roles. For example, AI might automate grammar checks, but teachers lead discussions on rhetorical nuance in Macbeth.

- Prioritise Evidence-Based Practices: AI should enhance proven methods like active learning and retrieval practice. Beware schools replacing essay writing with AI-generated content, which undermines cognitive development.

- Resist *The Magpie Effect*: VR headsets or chatbots earn their place only if tied to curriculum goals - e.g., simulating historical debates, not just virtual campus tours.

Red Flag: A school boasting "AI-driven personalised learning" but lacking teacher training in interpreting AI data.

Green Light: Professional development programmes where teachers learn to curate AI tools alongside classical pedagogy.

2. The Three Pillars of Responsible AI Integration

Pillar 1: Critical Thinkers, Not Consumers

Schools should foster learners who question AI outputs, not passively accept them. Look for curricula where:

- Learners audit AI-generated essays for logical fallacies.

- Philosophy classes debate AI ethics (e.g., "Can algorithms be impartial?").

Pillar 2: Tools, Not Crutches

AI should stretch creativity, not stifle it. Strong schools might:

- Use coding projects to demystify AI's workings (e.g., building simple chatbots).

- Ban AI for foundational tasks (essay drafting) but allow it for advanced synthesis (comparing AI and human translations of Homer).

Pillar 3: Equity Over Efficiency

AI must bridge gaps, not widen them. Ask:

- "How does the school support learners without home tech access?"

Parental Advocacy:

- Collaborate, Not Dictate: Support teacher expertise by joining committees reviewing AI tools, not prescribing classroom practices.
- Demand Transparency: Request clear documentation on how AI aligns with the school's mission and learner outcomes.

Schools as Guardians of Cognitive Sovereignty

The best schools treat AI as a chisel, not the sculptor; a tool to reveal human potential, not redefine it. Parents must seek institutions where technology amplifies the Trivium's rigour, ensuring learners emerge as masters of AI, not its subjects.

5. The Future of Learning is Classical and Technological

5: The Future of Learning is Classical and Technological

Dorothy Sayers' The Lost Tools of Learning diagnosed modern education's ailment as a fixation on answers and subjects over cognitive discipline. Were she to survey today's AI-disrupted classrooms, she might diagnose a new symptom: cognitive outsourcing; the delegation of thinking itself to machines. Yet her prescription would endure: utilise the Trivium's tripartite rigour. Imagine her arguing that AI, wisely harnessed, could be the very tool to resurrect the timeless model she championed. This would serve to develop learners who first master facts (Grammar), then dissect their relationships (Logic), and finally wield them persuasively (Rhetoric).

A Blueprint for Timeless Learning

For Parents: The task is to cultivate homes where technology serves rather than supplants effort. This begins with simple rules: AI checks homework only after unaided attempts, and devices stay silenced during family debates about history's ambiguities or science's open questions. Consider the parent who challenges their child to fact-check an AI-generated timeline of the Cold War, cross-referencing books and documentaries. Such acts transform gadgets from answer engines into debate partners.

For Educators: The classroom's future lies in treating AI as the new parchment, a medium for ideas, not their source. Teachers might deploy language models to generate deliberately flawed arguments about 1984's relevance, tasking learners with identifying logical gaps and rhetorical flabbiness. Meanwhile, AI's capacity to personalise maths drills could free instructors to mentor more and mark less, echoing Sayers' vision of educators as intellectual blacksmiths, not content delivery systems.

For Policymakers: Legislators must guard against the Magpie Effect in schools that leads to the hoarding of shiny tech without pedagogical intent. This means funding audits to ensure AI tools prioritise cognitive depth over convenience, and mandating "analog anchors" like compulsory handwriting until Year 9.

The Timeless Mission: Raising Thinkers

Education's highest calling is not to produce efficient employees for the AI economy, but sovereign thinkers who command technology because they first mastered their own minds. This demands resisting Silicon Valley's seductive narrative that faster, smarter tools equate to better learning. True progress lies in recognising that neurons cultivated through struggles (such as memorising poetry, wrestling with equations, defending contentious ideas) develop a resilience no algorithm can replicate.

History offers a stark lesson through the story of Imam Al-Ghazali, the 11th-century scholar whose caravan was ambushed by bandits. When a thief mocked him: "Your knowledge is worthless! It rides on the back of a donkey!", referring to his books, Al-Ghazali spent years committing his works to memory. His response embodies timeless learning's essence: knowledge must reside in the mind, not merely in external repositories. Today's "donkeys" are cloud servers and large-language models; indispensable, yet perilous if they become proxies for understanding.

The Alexandria Paradox looms large here. The ancient Library of Alexandria amassed scrolls but prioritised the verbal jousting of its scholars. Similarly, schools must balance AI's vast knowledge stores with Socratic sparring. A learner who uses a large-language model to summarise Plato's Republic but cannot debate its ethics over coffee has gained information, not wisdom.

The Timeless Learning Manifesto

Timeless Learning is neither a eulogy for the past nor a blind embrace of the future, but a clarion call to unite both:

We Will Not Outsource Wonder
From the first time a child asks "Why is the sky blue?" to the philosopher's quest for meaning, curiosity is humanity's birthright. AI can suggest answers, but it cannot kindle the spark of awe. This remains the work of parents reading bedtime stories, teachers igniting moments, and learners daring to question received truths.

We Will Equip, Not Replace
Let us wield AI as Michelangelo wielded his chisel: a tool to reveal the form within the marble, not to carve facsimiles of existing statues. This means apps that guide learners through the friction of mathematical proofs, not apps that solve equations for them; algorithms that personalise historical inquiry to deepen critique, not algorithms that draft essays on demand.

We Will Honour the Past to Build the Future

The Trivium is not a relic to museumise, but a living root system. Its Grammar Stage grounds learners in humanity's hard-won knowledge such as the laws of physics, the sonnets of Shakespeare, Hokusai's views of Mount Fuji. The Logic Stage trains them to interrogate AI's claims with the scepticism of Socrates. The Rhetoric Stage empowers them to persuade, not just prompt, shaping society's discourse rather than parroting its biases.

Dorothy Sayers closed her essay with a lament: "We let our young men and women go out unarmed in a day when armour was never so necessary." Today, the armour is not more technology, but the cognitive sovereignty to wield it wisely. The thinkers we raise will be those who ask, upon encountering an AI's flawless answer, "What question have we forgotten to ask?" They will be the architects of tomorrow's algorithms, the ethicists of its dilemmas, the poets of its possibilities. In answering Sayers' call to re-arm learners with the Trivium's tools, we gift them not just the mastery of machines, but the irreplaceable power to remain human in an age of automation.

Glossary

AI: Artificial Intelligence. This encompasses technologies designed to simulate human intelligence to complete tasks, such as learning, reasoning, problem-solving, perception, and language understanding. Key subfields include machine learning, natural language processing (NLP), computer vision, robotics, and expert systems.

Cognitive Load Theory: A psychological theory that explains how the brain's working memory processes information.

Dialectic: The art of investigating or discussing the truth of opinions. In the context of the Trivium, it is the second stage, focusing on logic and argumentation. It is a method of dealing with subjects, using language to define terms, make accurate statements, construct arguments, and detect fallacies. Dialectic embraces logic and disputation.

Dunning-Kruger Effect: A cognitive bias where people with low competence in a task overestimate their ability.

Germane Load: The productive effort of forming lasting skills.

Grammar: In the context of the Trivium, the first stage focuses on language and foundational knowledge.

Intrinsic Load: The inherent complexity of a task.

Logic: The study of the principles of reasoning.

Magpie Effect: The tendency of educators to be drawn to the latest technological tools that promise innovation but often fail to deliver meaningful learning outcomes.

Quadrivium: The second part of the medieval curriculum, focusing on subjects like arithmetic, geometry, music, and astronomy.

Rhetoric: The art of effective or persuasive speaking or writing. In the context of the Trivium, it is the third stage, focusing on expression and persuasion.

Trivium: The first part of the medieval curriculum, consisting of grammar, dialectic, and rhetoric.

* 9 7 8 1 0 3 6 9 1 7 0 3 6 *